My Annual Personal Almanac & Agenda 2024

My personal Almanac & Agenda 2024

Rightsideceo@ymail.com

Author

Liza Mitchell

lizam3547@gmail.com

Cover -Design and formatting

Sirazul I.@sirazul_19

Editor/ Project Manager

Felicia S. Cauley

Project Manager

Robert Cauley

Made in the United States of America

ISBN-978-1-955050-69-2

Right Side Publishing

P.O Box 336 Reynoldsburg Ohio

www.rightsidepublishing.com

Introduction

My Annual Personal Almanac & Agenda (MAPA&A) is a whole life planner that allows a monthly billing cycle and a biweekly pay period to coexist with your daily needs. It was designed to help plan out your entire year - one week at a time. There are just 168 hours between Sunday and Saturday. The best way to manage your time is to build a weekly schedule that you can stick to.

A typical schedule begins with working full time. Working at least 40 hours each week will maximize income and improve opportunities for advancement.

Most authorities on health and wellbeing recommend 30 minutes each of physical activity and prayer or meditation each day. Most people benefit from 7-8 hours of uninterrupted sleep every 24 hours.

If you work full time, sleep well and then take the time each day to pray and exercise, up to 103 hours of the 168-hour week will already be accounted for. With so many requirements of your time, how will you make use of those remaining 65 hours?

*Prepare meals

*Consume meals

*Clean house (daily, weekly, monthly, annual chores)

*Self-care - naps, showers, and hygiene, applying makeup, styling hair, personal services like going to the nail or hair salon or getting a massage

*Momming - any time devoted to your children to encourage their leisure, their personal care. (i.e., mealtimes, bathing, homework)

*Downtime is your free time to reasonably spend how you like

With the MAPA&A, you will have a well thought out approach to managing everything that falls between how you spend your time to how you spend your money. MAPA&A is meant to be kept as private as a diary, so be intentional with how you keep your records.

The MAPA&A contains two sections.

Section one (data collection and routine set up)

- **A daily to-do list and daily routine** helps to establish routines.
- **An annual to-do list and annual routine** helps to establish routines.
- **Annual medical appointment** scheduling for you and up to three children
- **Bi-Annual dental appointment** scheduling for you and up to three children
- **My home, family & vehicle incident report** To keep up with the details surrounding incidents (i.e., home or car repair issues, or any contact with local law enforcement at home or while away from home)
- **Expenses Guide** and **My Expenses Guide** list all the places that want money from you and the date it is typically due.
- **My Family's Shopping Guide** Every one of your family members has their own individuality. That typically means everyone prefers something different. Use My Family's Shopping Guide to keep track of all the things that would become a crisis if you do not remember.
- **My Family's Shopping Guide** Use the second page of My Family's Shopping Guide to update changes (sizes, favorite flavors) that may occur later in the year.
- **My Saving's Itinerary** Use the provided formula to figure out how long it will take and how much money to set aside to save for a large purchase.
- **My Doodling Vision Board** The doodling vision board is just like a regular vision board. But instead of gluing pages taken from a magazine, use pens and pencils to capture your vision in your own drawings. The effort you would normally use to find the items and concepts you want to strive for in various magazines, with the My Doodling Vision Board, use internet searches to find proper names and wordings. Then write what you find under the pictures you draw.

Section two (12 – Month Calendar)

- **Each calendar month will contain:**
- **Heading calendar** containing chosen calendar events

    Back page of **Heading calendar:** (Design Undecided)

    Option 1 - please remember and do not forget.

    Option 2 - leave it blank.

- **My Calendar** – Other than the numbers, the calendar is blank for the user to record pay periods, bill due dates, appointments, and upcoming events.
- **Monthly Routine** (i.e., My January Routine) helps to establish routines.
- **My Monthly Financial Obligations** – On the lines: 1st, 2nd, 3rd, 4th paycheck Date write your pay dates in order. Then, using the bills you listed in the My Expenses Guide from Section One, write one on each line under the corresponding pay period that will ensure payment will be submitted on time. Now that your bills have been laid out, it is time to plan meals and start a grocery list.
- **Monthly Meal Planner -** will help end food waste and curb excessive spending in the grocery store. Fresh foods are the healthiest foods, and the MAPA&A promotes consumption of fresher food by scheduling meal purchases to occur once every two weeks with intent to consume most of what is purchased. There are three spaces allotted each day for three meals. If you use the 6-meal method, just combine two meals in each space. Attempt to build meals using foods and products already on hand. Consuming what you have before purchasing anew will reduce potential waste, shorten the grocery list, and therefore reduce the grocery bill. Once at least fourteen meals are created, put your grocery list on The Paycheck Shopping List for all the items you do not already have.
- **Paycheck Shopping List** – to ensure the cost of the products your household is accustomed to having around the house is included in the overall budget.

You have now been equipped to execute the plans that you have carefully laid out. Now it is time to reflect by journaling.

- *My (Monthly) Journal Topic of the Month*
- *My (Monthly) Thoughts*

Daily to-do list

For your health and well-being

o 30 minutes of prayer/meditation

o 30 minutes of continuous physical activity/exercise

o Take medications/daily supplements.

o Use "Monthly Journal to write positive affirmations.

o Sanitize cellular devices and other similar items.

o Take frozen foods out of the freezer in the morning or night before to cook for dinner and thaw them in the refrigerator.

For your children's health and well-being

o Spend time with your children separately and then eat a meal together as a family, encouraging them to share their experiences with one another.

Check Email

o Open important emails; delete spam.

o Respond to each email.

o Delete all read emails.

o Empty Email account trash bin

Listen to voicemail messages

o Write down what is being communicated, if needed to remember

o Delete (or save) the message

Personal Accounting

o Account for all purchase receipts from bank card purchases to avoid NSF fees.

o Discard or file receipts (Only keep receipts in wallet for returns or legal purposes)

Check online Bank access.
o Keep a check register.
o Balance checkbook each day until all drafts have been cleared, then every few days

Delivered mail.
o Open and read each piece of mail no matter the sender, the destroy and discard or file.
o Record bill due dates on "My Calendar"

Self-Care
o Add your own.
o Add your own.
o Add your own.

Add your own.
o Add your own.
o Add your own.

Annual to-do list

- [ ] Schedule myself a physical exam
- [ ] Schedule myself a dental exam during the first half of the year
- [ ] Schedule myself a dental exam during the second half of the year
- [ ] Schedule each of the children a physical exam
- [ ] Schedule each of the children adental exam during the first half of the year
- [ ] chedule each of the children adental exam during the second half of the year
- [ ] Spring Clean
- [ ] Renew vehicle registration before mybirthday.
- [ ] Is this my year for a new ID/driver's license?
- [ ] File my taxes.
- [ ] Renew dog licenses (may have to first satisfy veterinary requirements)
- [ ] Perform a "State of my Life" now and every six months moving forward.
- [ ] Review your vehicle and renter's insurance policies, check for competitive rates.
- [ ] Fall Prepare
- [ ] Tune up the car before winter months begin.
- [ ] Change batteries in smoke alarms on the same day each year.
- [ ] Change batteries in carbon monoxide detectors on the same day each year.
- [ ] Add your own.
- [ ] Add your own.
- [ ] Add your own.
- [ ]
- [ ]
- [ ]

in my Annual Credit Reports & Scores

TransUnion - Credit Score_____ Date of Score _____

Experian - Credit Score _____ Date of Score _____

Equifax - Credit Score _____ Date of Score _____

My Daily Routine

On Sundays, I/we

On Mondays, I/we

On Tuesdays, I/we

On Wednesdays, I/we

On Thursdays, I/we

On Fridays, I/we

On Saturdays, I/we

My Annual Routine

In January, I/we	In February	In March

In April	In May	In June

My Annual Routine

In July	August	In September

In October	In November	In December

My Appointment

The date of my annual physical is: _____

(date of exam)

I will be seen by : _____

(Name and title of medical professional)

At _____

(Save the address & phone number of medical officeincell.)

Instructions for when I get to my doctor's office:

(Parking procedures, what building, what floor, where to sign in)

_____

_____

_____

_____

What I would like to discuss with the doctor during my appointment:

_____

_____

_____

_____

_____

_____

_____

Record Appointment

_____ First half of the year _____

Child #1   Date of Exam

_____ First half of the year _____

Child #2   Date of Exam

_____ First half of the year _____

Child #3   Date of Exam

_____ Second half of the year _____

Child #1   Date of Exam

_____ Second half of the year _____

Child #2   Date of Exam

_____ Second half of the year _____

Child #3   Date of Exam

Annual to-do list, Scheduling the children's medical appointments.

The children receive their annual physicals from:

_____

(Save address & phone number of medical office in cell.)

Instructions for when I get to their doctor's office:
(Parking procedures, what building, what floor, where to sign in)

_____

_____

_____

_____

_____

_____

_____

_____

_____

_____

_____

_____

_____

_____

_____

Annual to-do list, My January-June dental exam notes

My dental exam for the first half of the year is on _____

My January-June dental exam

Concerns to express with dentist:_____

_____

_____

_____

_____

_____

_____

_____

_____

The Dentist Suggests:

_____

_____

_____

_____

_____

_____

_____

Annual to-do list, My eldest child's annual physical exam notes

What I would like to discuss about my eldest child with their physician

_____

_____

_____

_____

_____

Weight _____   Height _____   Blood Pressure _____

The Doctor Suggests:

_____

_____

_____

_____

_____

_____

_____

_____

Referrals: _____

_____

_____

_____

Annual to-do list, My July-December dental exam notes

My dental exam for the second half of the year is on: _____

(date of exam)

My July-December dental exam

Concerns to express with the dentist: _____

_____

_____

_____

_____

_____

_____

_____

_____

The Dentist Suggests:

_____

_____

_____

_____

_____

_____

_____

Annual to-do list, My eldest child's January – June dental exam notes

What I need to discuss with dentist:

_____

_____

_____

_____

_____

_____

_____

Their January – June dental exam is on: _____

(date of exam)

The Dentist Suggests:

_____

_____

_____

_____

_____

_____

Referrals:

_____

_____

_____

Annual to-do list, My eldest child's July - December dental exam notes

What I need to discuss with the dentist:

_____

_____

_____

_____

_____

_____

_____

Their July - December dental exam is on : _____

(date of exam)

The Dentist Suggests:

_____

_____

_____

_____

_____

_____

Referrals:

_____

_____

_____

Annual to-do list, My second child's annual physical exam notes

What I would like to discuss about my second child with their physician

_____

_____

_____

_____

_____

_____

Weight _____   Height _____   Blood Pressure _____

The Doctor Suggests:

_____

_____

_____

_____

_____

_____

_____

Referrals:

_____

_____

_____

_____

Annual to-do list, My second child's January – June dental exam notes

What I need to discuss with dentist:

_____

_____

_____

_____

_____

_____

Their January – June dental exam is on: _____

(date of exam)

The Dentist Suggests:

_____

_____

_____

_____

_____

_____

Referrals:

_____

_____

_____

Annual to-do list, My second child's July - December dental exam notes

What I need to discuss with dentist:

_____
_____
_____
_____
_____
_____
_____

Their July - December dental exam is on: _____

(date of exam)

The Dentist Suggests:

_____
_____
_____
_____
_____
_____

Referrals:

_____
_____
_____

Annual to-do list, My third child's annual physical exam notes

What I would like to discuss about my third child with their physician

_____

_____

_____

_____

_____

_____

Weight _____   Height _____   Blood Pressure _____

The Doctor Suggests:

_____

_____

_____

_____

_____

_____

Referrals:

_____

_____

_____

_____

Annual to-do list, My third child's January – June dental exam notes

What I need to discuss with dentist:

_____
_____
_____
_____
_____
_____
_____

Their January – June dental exam is on: _____

(date of exam)

The Dentist Suggests:

_____
_____
_____
_____
_____
_____

Referrals:

_____
_____
_____

Annual to-do list, My third child's July - December dental exam notes

What I need to discuss with dentist:

_____

_____

_____

_____

_____

_____

Their July - December dental exam is on: _____

(date of exam)

The Dentist Suggests:

_____

_____

_____

_____

_____

_____

Referrals:

_____

_____

_____

	2024 Home, Family & Vehicle Incident Report	
	Date	Brief Description of Incident & Outcome
1		
2		
3		
4		
5		
6		
7		
8		

My Expenses Guide

Where does your money go? How much money comes in minus how much money is paid out in bills and how much it costs to manage your life equals money that can be spent on diversions and entertainment or hobbies. It can also be saved and invested. Here are the things people typically spend money on:

Charitable Contributions
- Church tithes
- Donate your resources
    - clothes
    - money
    - time

Insurances
- Homeowners or renters
- Life
- Medical
- Automobile

Housing
- Rent or mortgage.

Out of pocket medical expenses
- Medical supplies
- OTC meds
- Vitamins& Supplements

Childcare expenses

Pet expenses
- Food & treats
- Toys
- Veterinary & emergency expenses
- Grooming

Grocery budget
- Meals
- Snacks and soda
- Food to pack for work/school

Laundry services

Utilities
- Electric
- Gas
- Water
- Wi-Fi

Transportation
- Public transportation
- Uber
- Car note
- Insurance (recorded above)
- Fuel
- Maintenance& Upkeep
- Cleaning

Credit cards
- Credit card payments

Savings
- Vacation fund
- Emergency fund
- Car fund
- Kids fund

Personal grooming
- Hair styling
- Mani/Pedi
- Tanning

Service subscriptions
- Internet television
- Internet radio

Hobbies

Recreation & diversions
- Dining out
- Cigarettes & Alcohol

My Expenses Guide

	financial obligation	who do you pay this bill to?	Account #	Monthly amount
1	Housing			
2	Electricity			
3	Gas			
4	Water/Sewer			
5	City Trash Pick-Up			
6	Child Daycare			
7	Car Note			
8	Auto Insurance			
9	Renter's Insurance			
10	Life Insurance			
11	Cellular Phone			
12	WiFi Subscription			
13	Internet Television			
14	Music Streaming Service			
15				
16				
17				
18				
19				
20				
21				
22				

Shopping key for 1st half of year Jan - June

Shopping key for 1st half of year Jan - June	Name: _____	Name: _____	Name: _____	Name: _____	Name: _____
Allergy					
Allergy					
Disliked flavor/food					
Remember to never...					
Favorite color					
Second favorite color					
Favorite flavor					
Second favorite flavor					
shoe size & style					
sock size and style					
2nd shoe size & style					
2nd sock size and style					
hosiery size & style					

bra size & style					
conceal-wear size & style					
undershirt size and style					
underwear size & style					
tee shirt size & style					
2nd tee shirt size & style					
shirt size & style					
2nd type shirt size & style					
pants size & style					
2nd pants size & style					

Shopping key for 2nd half of year July - Dec

Shopping key for 2nd half of year July - Dec	Name: _____	Name: _____	Name: _____	Name: _____	Name: _____
Allergy					
Allergy					
Disliked flavor/food					
Remember to never...					
Favorite color					
Second favorite color					
Favorite flavor					
Second favorite flavor					
shoe size & style					
sock size and style					
2nd shoe size & style					
2nd sock size and style					
hosiery size & style					

bra size & style					
conceal-wear size & style					
undershirt size and style					
underwear size & style					
tee shirt size & style					
2nd tee shirt size & style					
shirt size & style					
2nd type shirt size & style					
pants size & style					
2nd pants size & style					

Planning to Purchase Items by Saving from Each Paycheck

Item	(A) Total Cost of Item	Target Purchase Date	(B) # of pay periods away	(A)/(B) = Amount to save each pay in order to purchase item	Saving Start Date
EXAMPLE: Studio grade Audio Interface with Microphone and stand	$1,450.00	In about months	10	$1450÷10 = $140.00	Which pay period will you begin your savings plan?

Planning to Purchase Items by Saving from Each Paycheck

Item	(A) Total Cost of Item	Target Purchase Date	(B) # of pay periods away	(A)/(B) = Amount to save each pay in order to purchase item	Saving Start Date
EXAMPLE: Studio grade Audio Interface with Microphone and stand	$1,450.00	In about months	10	$1450÷10 = $140.00	Which pay period will you begin your savings plan?

Vision board for personal growth
If I dare to dream big, I can....
Vision Board for Personal Growth
If I dare to dream BIG, I can:

___

Having a vision takes planning, consideration and action.

Is this vision financially plausible?

What makes this vision attainable?

What is needed outside of my own knowledge and experience in order for this vision to be accomplished?

What do I need to do to get started?

How will my current life suffer? What will be the recoup for the loss? What will keep me moving forward?

When do I expect my reward to come? What do I expect my reward to be?

If the arrival of my reward is delayed, can I promise myself to not allow the discouragement to deter me?

Can I, also, make the promise to never quit no matter how much of my regular life monopolizes the time I wish that I could spend on my vision?

Vision Board for Personal Growth

If I dare to dream BIG...

Vision Board for Personal Growth

If I dare to dream big,

I can. . ..

January 2024

Flowers: Carnation & Snowdrop   **Birthstone: Garnet**

Sunday	Monday	Tuesday	Wednesday	Thursday	Friday	Saturday
31-Dec	**1** **New Years Day** <> Polar Bear Plunge Day <> **National Hangover Day**	**2** Buffet Day <> Science Fiction Day	**3** Fruitcake Toss Day <> Festival of Sleep Day	**4** Trivia Day	**5** Bird Day	**6** Bean Day
7 National Black HIV/AIDS Awareness Day <> Old Rock Day <> Naitonal Bobblehead Day	**8** Earth's Rotation Day <> National Bubble Bath Day	**9** Naitonal Shop for Travel Day <> Static Electricity Day <> Word Nerd Day <> Clean off Your Desk Day	**10** Harriet Tubman Day <> Cut your Energy costs Day <>	**11** Learn your Name in Morse Code Day	**12** Marizipan Day	**13** Make your Dreams come True Day <> Rubber Ducky Day <> Sticker Day
14 Organize your Home Day <> Kite Day	**15** **Martin Luther King, Jr Day** <> Strawberry Ice Cream Day <> Bagel & Lox Day	**16** Religious Freedom Day <> Nothing Day	**17** Benjamin Franklin Day <> Kid Inventors Day <> Ditch your New Years Resolutions Day	**18** Thesaurus Day <> Tin Can Day	**19** National Day of Honor <> Capricorn ends <> Popcorn Day	**20** Aquarius begins <> Penguin Awareness Day
21 National Sanctity of Human Life Day <> World Religion Day <> Soup Swap Day <> Squirrel Appreciation Day	**22** Hot Sauce Day <> Answer your cat's questions Day	**23** Handwriting Day	**24** MacIntosh Computer Day <> National Compliment Day	**25** Greek Independence Day <> Opposite Day	**26** International Customs Day <> Spouse' Day	**27** Chocolate Cake Day
28 World Leprosy Day <> National Kazoo Day	**29** National Vietnam War Veterans Day <> National Puzzle Day	**30** National Draw a Dinosaur Day <> Croissant Day	**31** Transgender Day of Visibility <> Backwards Day	1-Feb	2-Feb	3-Feb

National Blood Donor Month <> Thyroid Awareness Month <> Dry January <> Slavery & Human Trafficking Prevention Month <> National Mentoring Month

My January 2024

Sunday	Monday	Tuesday	Wednesday	Thursday	Friday	Saturday
31-Dec	1	2	3	4	5	6
7	8	9	10	11	12	13
14	15	16	17	18	19	20
21	22	23	24	25	26	27
28	29	30	31	1-Feb	2-Feb	3-Feb

My January Financial Obligations

List bills due after this paydate but before the next paydate

1st Paycheck Date_____	Bill Due Date	Bill Amount
Financial Obligation		
1		
2		
3		
4		
5		
6		
7		
8		

My January Financial Obligations

List bills due after this paydate but before the next paydate

2nd Paycheck Date_____	Bill Due Date	Bill Amount
Financial Obligation		
9		
10		
11		
12		
13		
14		
15		
16		

My January Financial Obligations

List bills due after this paydate but before the next paydate

3rd Paycheck Date_____		Bill Due Date	Bill Amount
	Financial Obligation		
1			
2			
3			
4			
5			
6			
7			
8			

My January Financial Obligations

List bills due after this paydate but before the next paydate

4th Paycheck Date_____		Bill Due Date	Bill Amount
	Financial Obligation		
9			
10			
11			
12			
13			
14			
15			
16			

January Meal Planner

	Breakfast or Brunch	Lunch	Afternoon Snack	Dinner
31-Dec				
1-Jan				
2-Jan				
3-Jan				
4-Jan				
5-Jan				
6-Jan				
7-Jan				
8-Jan				
9-Jan				
10-Jan				
11-Jan				

January Meal Planner

	Breakfast or Brunch	Lunch	Afternoon Snack	Dinner
12-Jan				
13-Jan				
14-Jan				
15-Jan				
16-Jan				
17-Jan				
18-Jan				
19-Jan				
20-Jan				
21-Jan				
22-Jan				
23-Jan				

January Meal Planner

	Breakfast or Brunch	Lunch	Afternoon Snack	Dinner
24-Jan				
25-Jan				
26-Jan				
27-Jan				
28-Jan				
29-Jan				
30-Jan				
31-Jan				

My January First Paycheck Shopping List

Household Products	Personal Products	Ingredients for Planned Meals

My January Second Paycheck Shopping List

Household Products	Personal Products	Ingredients for Planned Meals

My January Third Paycheck Shopping List

Household Products	Personal Products	Ingredients for Planned Meals

My January Foure Paycheck Shopping List

Household Products	Personal Products	Ingredients for Planned Meals

January Journal Topic of the Month:
Recap last year. How will this year be better than last year, even if last year was great.

_____

_____

_____

_____

_____

_____

_____

_____

_____

_____

_____

_____

_____

_____

_____

_____

_____

_____

_____

_____

_____

My January Thoughts:

_____

_____

_____

_____

_____

_____

_____

_____

_____

_____

_____

_____

_____

_____

_____

_____

_____

_____

_____

_____

Febraury 2024

Flowers: Violet, Iris & Primrose   **Birthstone: Amethyst**

Sunday	Monday	Tuesday	Wednesday	Thursday	Friday	Saturday
28-Jan	29-Jan	30-Jan	31-Jan	1	2 World Wetlands Day <> Day of the Crepe <> Play your Ukele Day	3 Ice Cream for Breakfast Day <> Thank your Mailman Day
4 World Cancer Day	5 National Weatherperson's Day <> Chocolate Fondue Day	6	7 Congenital Heart Defect Awareness Week <> National Black HIV/AIDS Awareness Day	8 Kite Flying Day	9 Tootheache Day <> Bagel & Lox Day	10 Umbrella Day
11 World Day of the Sick <> Don't Cry Over Spilled Milk	12 Darwin Day	13 Mardi Gras <> Shrove Tuesday <> Clean Out your Computer Day <> Radio Day	14 Valentine's Day <> Ferris Wheel Day <> Library Lovers Day	15 Susan B. Anthony Day <> Gumdrop Day	16 Do a Grouch a Favor	17 Random Act of Kindness Day
18 Aquarius ends <> Battery Day	19 President's Day<> Pisces begins <> Tug of War Day <> Chocolate Mint Day	20	21	22 Single Tasking Day <> Be Humble Day	23 Dog biscuit appreciation Day	24 Tortilla Chip Day
25 Sword Swallowers Day	26 Tell a Fairy Tale Day	27 Polar Bear Day <> No Brainer Day	28 Tooth Fairy Day <> Public Sleeping Day	29 Leap Day	1-Mar	2-Mar

Black History Month <> American Heart Month <> National Bird-Feeding Month <> National Cancer Prevention Month

My Febraury 2024

Sunday	Monday	Tuesday	Wednesday	Thursday	Friday	Saturday
28-Jan	29-Jan	30-Jan	31-Jan	1	2	3
4	5	6	7	8	9	10
11	12	13	14	15	16	17
18	19	20	21	22	23	24
25	26	27	28	29	1-Mar	2-Mar

My February Routine

On Sundays, I/We:

On Mondays, I/We

On Tuesdays, I/We

On Wednesdays, I/We

On Thursdays, I/We

On Fridays, I/We

On Saturdays, I/We

My February Financial Obligations

List bills due after this paydate but before the next paydate

1st Paycheck Date_____	Bill Due Date	Bill Amount
Financial Obligation		
1		
2		
3		
4		
5		
6		
7		
8		

My February Financial Obligations

List bills due after this paydate but before the next paydate

2nd Paycheck Date_____	Bill Due Date	Bill Amount
Financial Obligation		
9		
10		
11		
12		
13		
14		
15		
16		

My February Financial Obligations

List bills due after this paydate but before the next paydate

3rd Paycheck Date_____	Bill Due Date	Bill Amount
Financial Obligation		
1		
2		
3		
4		
5		
6		
7		
8		

My February Financial Obligations

List bills due after this paydate but before the next paydate

4th Paycheck Date_____	Bill Due Date	Bill Amount
Financial Obligation		
9		
10		
11		
12		
13		
14		
15		
16		

February Meal Planner

	Breakfast or Brunch	Lunch	Afternoon Snack	Dinner
1-Feb				
2-Feb				
3-Feb				
4-Feb				
5-Feb				
6-Feb				
7-Feb				
8-Feb				
9-Feb				
10-Feb				
11-Feb				
12-Feb				

February Meal Planner

	Breakfast or Brunch	Lunch	Afternoon Snack	Dinner
13-Feb				
14-Feb				
15-Feb				
16-Feb				
17-Feb				
18-Feb				
19-Feb				
20-Feb				
21-Feb				
22-Feb				
23-Feb				
24-Feb				

February Meal Planner

	Breakfast or Brunch	Lunch	Afternoon Snack	Dinner
25-Feb				
26-Feb				
27-Feb				
28-Feb				
29-Feb				

My February First Paycheck Shopping List

Household Products	Personal Products	Ingredients for Planned Meals

My February Second Paycheck Shopping List

Household Products	Personal Products	Ingredients for Planned Meals

My February Third Paycheck Shopping List

Household Products	Personal Products	Ingredients for Planned Meals

My February Foure Paycheck Shopping List

Household Products	Personal Products	Ingredients for Planned Meals

_____

_____

_____

_____

_____

_____

_____

_____

_____

_____

_____

_____

_____

_____

_____

_____

_____

_____

_____

_____

_____

My February Thoughts:

March 2024

Flowers: Gladiolus & Poppy　　　　　**Birthstone: Larkspur**

Sunday	Monday	Tuesday	Wednesday	Thursday	Friday	Saturday
25-Feb	26-Feb	27-Feb	28-Feb	Feb-29	1 Self-Injury Awareness Day <> Compliment Day	2 Old Stuff Day
3 I want you to be Happy Day	4 March Forth & do Something Day <> Toy Soldier Day	5 Learn What your Name Means Day	6 Dentist's Day	7 Alexander Graham Bell Day <> Sock Monkey Day	8 Proofreading Day	9 Barbie Day
10 Harriet Tubman Day <> Daylight Savings Time begins	11 Oatmean Nut Waffle Day	12 Alfred Hitchcock Day	13 Napping Day <> Jewel Day <> Ken Day	14 World Kidney Day <> Pi Day	15 Long Covid Awareness Day	16 Incredible Kid Day
17 **St Patrick's Day** <> Submarine Day	18 Awkward Moments Day	19 National Day of Honor <> *Spring Begins* <> Pisces ends	20 Aries begins <> Storytelling Day	21 Common Courtesy Day	22 Goof off Day	23 Earth Hour
24 Chocolate Covered Raisin Day	25 Greek Independence Day <> Waffle Day	26 Purple Day for Epiliepsy Awareness <>	27 Spanish Paella Day	28 Something on a Stick Day	29 National Vietnam War Veterans Day	30 National Doctor's Day <> Take a Walk in a Park Day
31 **Easter** <> International Transgender Day of Visibility <> Bunsen Burner Day	1-Apr	2-Apr	3-Apr	4-Apr	5-Apr	6-Apr

Irish - American Heritage Month <> Mustache March <> National Colon Cancer Awareness Month <> Women's History Month <> Youth Art Month <> Multiple Sclerosis Awareness Month <> National Bleeding Disorders Awareness Month <> National Kidney Month <> National TBI Awareness Month

March 2024

Sunday	Monday	Tuesday	Wednesday	Thursday	Friday	Saturday
25-Feb	26-Feb	27-Feb	28-Feb	Feb-29	1	2
3	4	5	6	7	8	9
10	11	12	13	14	15	16
17	18	19	20	21	22	23
24	25	26	27	28	29	30
31	1-Apr	2-Apr	3-Apr	4-Apr	5-Apr	6-Apr

My March Routine

On Sundays, I/We:

On Mondays, I/We

On Tuesdays, I/We

On Wednesdays, I/We

On Thursdays, I/We

On Fridays, I/We

On Saturdays, I/We

My March Financial Obligations

List bills due after this paydate but before the next paydate

1st Paycheck Date_____	Bill Due Date	Bill Amount
Financial Obligation		
1		
2		
3		
4		
5		
6		
7		
8		

My March Financial Obligations

List bills due after this paydate but before the next paydate

2nd Paycheck Date_____	Bill Due Date	Bill Amount
Financial Obligation		
9		
10		
11		
12		
13		
14		
15		
16		

My March Financial Obligations

List bills due after this paydate but before the next paydate

3rd Paycheck Date_____	Bill Due Date	Bill Amount
Financial Obligation		
1		
2		
3		
4		
5		
6		
7		
8		

My March Financial Obligations

List bills due after this paydate but before the next paydate

4th Paycheck Date_____		
Financial Obligation	**Bill Due Date**	**Bill Amount**
9		
10		
11		
12		
13		
14		
15		
16		

March Meal Planner

	Breakfast or Brunch	Lunch	Afternoon Snack	Dinner
1-Mar				
2-Mar				
3-Mar				
4-Mar				
5-Mar				
6-Mar				
7-Mar				
8-Mar				
9-Mar				
10-Mar				
11-Mar				
12-Mar				

March Meal Planner

	Breakfast or Brunch	Lunch	Afternoon Snack	Dinner
13-Mar				
14-Mar				
15-Mar				
16-May				
17-Mar				
18-Mar				
19-Mar				
20-Mar				
21-Mar				
22-Mar				
23-Mar				
24-Mar				

March Meal Planner

	Breakfast or Brunch	Lunch	Afternoon Snack	Dinner
25-Mar				
26-Mar				
27-Mar				
28-Mar				
29-Mar				
30-Mar				
31-Mar				

My March First Paycheck Shopping List

Household Products	Personal Products	Ingredients for Planned Meals

My March Second Paycheck Shopping List

Household Products	Personal Products	Ingredients for Planned Meals

My March Third Paycheck Shopping List

Household Products	Personal Products	Ingredients for Planned Meals

My March Foure Paycheck Shopping List

Household Products	Personal Products	Ingredients for Planned Meals

March Journal Topic of the Month:
Kermit the Frog once sang"It's Not Easy Being Green
" What makes you a unique individual?

_____

_____

_____

_____

_____

_____

_____

_____

_____

_____

_____

_____

_____

_____

_____

_____

_____

_____

_____

_____

_____

_____

My March Thoughts:

April 2024

Flowers: Sweet Pea & Daisy　　　　**Birthstone: Diamond**

Sunday	Monday	Tuesday	Wednesday	Thursday	Friday	Saturday
31-Mar	1 April Fool's Day <> National Public Health Week (1st - 7th)	2	3 Party Day	4	5 First Conact Day <> Read a Road Map Day	6 Tartan Day <> Sorry Charlie Day
7 No Housework Day <> Walk to Work Day	8 Draw a Picture of a Bird Day	9 National Former P.O.W. Recognition Day <> Unicorn Day	10 Youth HIV/AIDS Awareness Day <> Siblings Day	11 National D.A.R.E. Day <> Submarine Day	12 Walk on Your Wild Side Day	13 Scrabble Day
14 Pan-American Day <> Pan-American Week <> Moment of Laughter Day	15 World Art Day <> *Tax Day* <> Eggs Benedict Day	16 Wear Your Pajamas to Work Day	17 Haiku Poetry Day	18 Education & Sharing Day <> International Day for Monuments & Sites <> Aries ends <> Pinata Day	19 Taurus begins	20 Look alike Day
21	22 Jelly Bean Day	23 Take a Chance Day <> Impossible Astronaut Day <>Lover's Day	24	25 DNA Day	26 Richter Scale Day	27 Take our daughters & sons to work Day
28	29 Dance Day <> Astronomy Day <> Zipper Day	30 Bugs Bunny Day <> Honesty Day	1-May	2-May	3-May	4-May

Irritable Bowel Syndrome Awareness Month <> National Autism Awareness Month <> National Child Abuse Prevention Month <> National Donate Life Month <> National Minority Health Month <> National Parkinsons Awareness Month <> Arab-American Heritage Month <> Financial Literacy Month <> Jazz Appreciation Month <> Math Awareness Month <> Cancer Contol Month <> Confederate History Month <> Dalit History Month <> National Poetry & Poetry Writing Month <>National Volunteer Month <> School Library Month <> Second Chance Month <> Sexual Assault Awareness Month

My April 2024

Sunday	Monday	Tuesday	Wednesday	Thursday	Friday	Saturday
31-Mar	1	2	3	4	5	6
7	8	9	10	11	12	13
14	15	16	17	18	19	20
21	22	23	24	25	26	27
28	29	30	31	1-May	2-May	3-May

My April Routine

On Sundays, I/We:

On Mondays, I/We

On Tuesdays, I/We

On Wednesdays, I/We

On Thursdays, I/We

On Fridays, I/We

On Saturdays, I/We

My April Financial Obligations

List bills due after this paydate but before the next paydate

1st Paycheck Date_____		Bill Due Date	Bill Amount
	Financial Obligation		
1			
2			
3			
4			
5			
6			
7			
8			

My April Financial Obligations

List bills due after this paydate but before the next paydate

2nd Paycheck Date_____		Bill Due Date	Bill Amount
	Financial Obligation		
9			
10			
11			
12			
13			
14			
15			
16			

My April Financial Obligations

List bills due after this paydate but before the next paydate

3rd Paycheck Date_____	Bill Due Date	Bill Amount
Financial Obligation		
1		
2		
3		
4		
5		
6		
7		
8		

My April Financial Obligations

List bills due after this paydate but before the next paydate

4th Paycheck Date_____	Bill Due Date	Bill Amount
Financial Obligation		
9		
10		
11		
12		
13		
14		
15		
16		

April Meal Planner

	Breakfast or Brunch	Lunch	Afternoon Snack	Dinner
1-Apr				
2-Apr				
3-Apr				
4-Apr				
5-Apr				
6-Apr				
7-Apr				
8-Apr				
9-Apr				
10-Apr				
11-Apr				
12-Apr				

April Meal Planner

	Breakfast or Brunch	Lunch	Afternoon Snack	Dinner
13-Apr				
14-Apr				
15-Apr				
16-Apr				
17-Apr				
18-Apr				
19-Apr				
20-Apr				
21-Apr				
22-Apr				
23-Apr				
24-Apr				

April Meal Planner

	Breakfast or Brunch	Lunch	Afternoon Snack	Dinner
25-Apr				
26-Apr				
27-Apr				
28-Apr				
29-Apr				
30-Apr				

My April First Paycheck Shopping List

Household Products	Personal Products	Ingredients for Planned Meals

My April Second Paycheck Shopping List

Household Products	Personal Products	Ingredients for Planned Meals

My April Third Paycheck Shopping List

Household Products	Personal Products	Ingredients for Planned Meals

My April Foure Paycheck Shopping List

Household Products	Personal Products	Ingredients for Planned Meals

April Journal Topic of the Month:

April showers bring May flowers. What sacrifices can you make to help improve your current circumstances.

_____

_____

_____

_____

_____

_____

_____

_____

_____

_____

_____

_____

_____

_____

_____

_____

_____

_____

_____

My April Thoughts:

_____
_____
_____
_____
_____
_____
_____
_____
_____
_____
_____
_____
_____
_____
_____
_____
_____
_____
_____
_____
_____
_____

May 2024

Flower: Lily of the Valley   **Birthstone: Emerald**

Sunday	Monday	Tuesday	Wednesday	Thursday	Friday	Saturday
28-Apr	29-Apr	30-Apr	**1** Loyalty Day <> Law Day <> Batman Day	**2** National Day of Prayer	**3**	**4** Beer Pong Day <> Star Wars Day
5 Cinco De Mayo <> Teacher Appreciation Week (5th - 11th) <> Family Equality Day <> No pants Day <> Laughter Day	**6** Herb Day <> Free Comic Book Day <> Beverage Day	**7** Teacher Appreciation Day	**8** World Ovarian Cancer Day <> World Red Cross & Red Crescent Day	**9** Food Allergy Awareness Week (9th - 15th) <> Europe Day <> Lost Sock Memorial Day	**10** Military Spouse's Day <> School Nurse Day <> Clean Up Your Room Day	**11** Miniture Golf Day <> Twilight Zone Day <> Eat What you Want Day
12 Mother's Day <> International Nurses Day <> Limerick Day	**13** Frog Jumping Day	**14** Moment of Laughter Day <> Reach as high as you Can Day <> Look up at the sky Day <> Dance Like a Chicken Day	**15** Peace Officer's Memorial Day <> Chocolate Chip Day	**16** Drawing Day	**17** National Defense Transportation Day & National Transportation Week <> Pizza Party Day <> Rat Pack Day	**18** Armed Forces Day <> No Dirty Dishes Day
19 Taurus ends <> Take your Parents to the Playground Day	**20** World Auto-Immune & Auto-Inflammatory Arthritis Day <> Gemini begins <> Be a Millionaire Day	**21** Talk Like Yoda Day	**22** National Maritime Day <> Solitaire Day <> Buy a Musical Instrument Day	**23** Lucky Penny Day	**24** Scavenger Hunt Day	**25** National Missing Children's Day <> African Liberation Day <> Sing Out Day <> Towel Day
26 Paper Airplane Day	**27** Memorial Day <> Grape Popscicle Day <> Sunscreen Day	**28** Hamburger Day	**29** Put a pillow on your Fridge Day	**30** Hole in my Bucket Day	**31** Smile Day <> Macaroon Day	1-Jun

Hatian Heritage Month <> Jewish-American Heritage Month <> Celiac Disease Awareness Month <> Asian-Pacific American Heritage Month <> Lyme Disease Awareness Month <> ALS Awareness Month <> Borderline Personality Disorder Awareness Month <> Brain Tumor Awareness Month <> Mental Health Awareness Month & Children's Mental Health Awareness Month <> National Bike Month <> National Military Appreciation Month <> National Foster Care Month <> National Pet Month <> National Stroke Awareness Month <> Zombie Awareness Month <> Arthritis Awareness Month <> Better Hearing & Speech Month <> Cystic Fibrosis Awareness Month <> Health Vision Month <> Hepatitis Awareness Month <> Lupus Awareness Month <> Skin Cancer Detection & Prevention Awareness Month <> National Asthma & Allergy Awareness Month <> National Physical Fitness & Sports Month <> Food Allergy Awareness Month

My May 2024

Sunday	Monday	Tuesday	Wednesday	Thursday	Friday	Saturday
28-Apr	29-Apr	30-Apr	1-May	2-May	3-May	4-May
5-May	6-May	7-May	8-May	9-May	10-May	11-May
12-May	13-May	14-May	15-May	16-May	17-May	18-May
19-May	20-May	21-May	22-May	23-May	24-May	25-May
26-May	27-May	28-May	29-May	30-May	1-Jun	2-Jun

My May Routine

On Sundays, I/We:

On Mondays, I/We

On Tuesdays, I/We

On Wednesdays, I/We

On Thursdays, I/We

On Fridays, I/We

On Saturdays, I/We

My May Financial Obligations

List bills due after this paydate but before the next paydate

1st Paycheck Date_____ Financial Obligation	Bill Due Date	Bill Amount
1		
2		
3		
4		
5		
6		
7		
8		

My May Financial Obligations

List bills due after this paydate but before the next paydate

2nd Paycheck Date_____ Financial Obligation	Bill Due Date	Bill Amount
9		
10		
11		
12		
13		
14		
15		
16		

My May Financial Obligations

List bills due after this paydate but before the next paydate

3rd st Paycheck Date_____	Bill Due Date	Bill Amount
Financial Obligation		
1		
2		
3		
4		
5		
6		
7		
8		

My May Financial Obligations

List bills due after this paydate but before the next paydate

4th Paycheck Date_____	Bill Due Date	Bill Amount
Financial Obligation		
9		
10		
11		
12		
13		
14		
15		
16		

May Meal Planner

	Breakfast or Brunch	Lunch	Afternoon Snack	Dinner
1-May				
2-May				
3-May				
4-May				
5-May				
6-May				
7-May				
8-May				
9-May				
10-May				
11-May				
12-May				

May Meal Planner

	Breakfast or Brunch	Lunch	Afternoon Snack	Dinner
13-May				
14-May				
15-May				
16-May				
17-May				
18-May				
19-May				
20-May				
21-May				
22-May				
23-May				
24-May				

May Meal Planner

	Breakfast or Brunch	Lunch	Afternoon Snack	Dinner
25-May				
26-May				
27-May				
28-May				
29-May				
30-May				
31-May				

My May First Paycheck Shopping List

Household Products	Personal Products	Ingredients for Planned Meals

My May Second Paycheck Shopping List

Household Products	Personal Products	Ingredients for Planned Meals

My May Third Paycheck Shopping List

Household Products	Personal Products	Ingredients for Planned Meals

My May Foure Paycheck Shopping List

Household Products	Personal Products	Ingredients for Planned Meals

May Journal Topic of the Month:
choose your topic
What is the best memory you can remember of you and your mother -or- What was your best defining moment as a mother? -or- Describe that one day that was a mother.

_____

_____

_____

_____

_____

_____

_____

_____

_____

_____

_____

_____

_____

_____

_____

_____

_____

_____

_____

My May Thoughts:

_____

_____

_____

_____

_____

_____

_____

_____

_____

_____

_____

_____

_____

_____

_____

_____

_____

_____

_____

_____

June 2024

Flower: Rose & Honeysuckle   **Birthstone: Pearl**

Sunday	Monday	Tuesday	Wednesday	Thursday	Friday	Saturday
26-May	27-May	28-May	29-May	30-May	31-May	1-Jun Tablecloth Day <> Say Something Nice Day
2-Jun Bubba Day	3-Jun National Child's Day <> Repeat Day	4-Jun Hug your Cat Day	5-Jun	6-Jun National Cancer Survivors Day <> Yo-yo Day <> Drive-in Movies Day	7-Jun	8-Jun Upsie-Daisy Day <> Doll Day <> Best Friends Day
9-Jun Donald Duck Day	10-Jun Iced Tea Day	11-Jun Corn on the Cob Day	12-Jun Family Health & Fitness Day <> Red Rose Day	13-Jun Sewing Machine Day	14-Jun **Flag Day** <> National Flag Week <> Bath Day <> Bourbon Day	15-Jun Juggling Day <> Nature Photography Day
16-Jun **Father's Day** <> Bloomsday	17-Jun Juggling Day	18-Jun Autistic Pride Day <> Splurge Day <> Picnic Day <> Panic Day	19-Jun **Juneenth** <> Gemini ends <> Garfield the Cat Day <> Sauntering Day	20-Jun **Summer Solstice** <> Cancer begins	21-Jun Selfie Day	22-Jun Onion Ring Day
23-Jun Typewriter Day	24-Jun Fairy Day	25-Jun Leon Day <> Please Take my Children to Work Day	26-Jun Chocolate Pudding Day	27-Jun Hellen Keller Day	28-Jun	29-Jun Camera Day
30-Jun Meteor Watch Day	1-Jul	2-Jul	3-Jul	4-Jul	5-Jul	6-Jul

National Safety Month <> Scoliosis Awareness Month <> (LGBT) Pride Month <> African-American Music Appreciation Month <> Caribbean-American Heritage Month

My June 2024

Sunday	Monday	Tuesday	Wednesday	Thursday	Friday	Saturday
26-May	27-May	28-May	29-May	30-May	31-May	1-Jun
2	3	4	5	6	7	8
9	10	11	12	13	14	15
16	17	18	19	20	21	22
23	24	25	26	27	28-Jan	29-Jan
30-Jun	1-Jul	2-Jul	3-Jul	4-Jul	5-Jul	6-Jul

My June Routine

On Sundays, I/We:

On Mondays, I/We

On Tuesdays, I/We

On Wednesdays, I/We

On Thursdays, I/We

On Fridays, I/We

On Saturdays, I/We

My June Financial Obligations

List bills due after this paydate but before the next paydate

1st Paycheck Date_____ Financial Obligation	Bill Due Date	Bill Amount
1		
2		
3		
4		
5		
6		
7		
8		

My June Financial Obligations

List bills due after this paydate but before the next paydate

2nd Paycheck Date_____ Financial Obligation	Bill Due Date	Bill Amount
9		
10		
11		
12		
13		
14		
15		
16		

My June Financial Obligations

List bills due after this paydate but before the next paydate

3rd Paycheck Date_____	Bill Due Date	Bill Amount
Financial Obligation		
1		
2		
3		
4		
5		
6		
7		
8		

My June Financial Obligations

List bills due after this paydate but before the next paydate

4th Paycheck Date_____	Bill Due Date	Bill Amount
Financial Obligation		
9		
10		
11		
12		
13		
14		
15		
16		

June Meal Planner

	Breakfast or Brunch	Lunch	Afternoon Snack	Dinner
1-Jun				
2-Jun				
3-Jun				
4-Jun				
5-Jun				
6-Jun				
7-Jun				
8-Jun				
9-Jun				
10-Jun				
11-Jun				
12-Jun				

June Meal Planner

	Breakfast or Brunch	Lunch	Afternoon Snack	Dinner
13-Jun				
14-Jun				
15-Jun				
16-Jun				
17-Jun				
18-Jun				
19-Jun				
20-Jun				
21-Jun				
22-Jun				
23-Jun				
24-Jun				

June Meal Planner

	Breakfast or Brunch	Lunch	Afternoon Snack	Dinner
25-Jun				
26-Jun				
27-Jun				
28-Jun				
29-Jun				
30-Jun				

My June First Paycheck Shopping List

Household Products	Personal Products	Ingredients for Planned Meals

My June Second Paycheck Shopping List

Household Products	Personal Products	Ingredients for Planned Meals

My June Third Paycheck Shopping List

Household Products	Personal Products	Ingredients for Planned Meals

My June Foure Paycheck Shopping List

Household Products	Personal Products	Ingredients for Planned Meals

What kind of life am I living? What am I doing when I am at my happiest?

_____

_____

_____

_____

_____

_____

_____

_____

_____

_____

_____

_____

_____

_____

_____

_____

_____

_____

_____

My June Thoughts:

July 2024

Flower: Larkspur & Waterlily   **Birthstone: Ruby**

Sunday	Monday	Tuesday	Wednesday	Thursday	Friday	Saturday
30-Jun	1 Joke Day	2 I Forgot Day <> UFO Day	3 Compliment Your Mirror Day <> Plastic Bag Free Day	4 **Independence Day** <> Sidewalk Egg Frying Day	5 Workholic Day	6 World Kissing Day
7 Tell the Truth Day	8 Video Games Day <> Math 2.0 Day	9 Sugar Cookie Day	10 Teddy Bear's Picnic Day	11 Swimming Pool Day <> Cheer Up the Lonely Day	12 Eat Your Jello Day <> Simplicity Day	13 Embrace Your Geekness Day
14 Pandemonium Day	15 Gummy Worm Day	16 Corn Fritters Day <> Ice Cream Day	17 Emoji Day <> Yellow Pig Day	18 Insurance Nerd Day <> Caviar Day	19 Stick Out Your Tongue Day	20 Chess Day <> Fortune Cookie Day <> Space Exploration Day
21 Cancer ends <> Junk Food Day	22 Leo begins <> Hammock Day <> PI Approximation Day	23 Vanilla Ice Cream Day	24 Cousins Day	25 Carousel Day <> Culinarians Day	26 Uncle & Aunt Day	27 National Korean War Veterans Armistice Day <> Walk on Stilts Day
28 Parent's Day <> Water Park Day <> Milk Chocolate Day	29 Lasagne Day	30 Cheesecake Day	31 Uncommon Musical Instrument Day	1-Aug	2-Aug	3-Aug

National Ice Cream Month <> Disability Pride Month <> Juvenile Arthritis Awareness Month <> National Cleft & Craniofacial Awareness & Prevention Month <> Sarcoma Awareness Month

My July 2024

Sunday	Monday	Tuesday	Wednesday	Thursday	Friday	Saturday
30-Jun	1	2	3	4	5	6
7	8	9	10	11	12	13
14	15	16	17	18	19	20
21	22	23	24	25	26	27
28	29	30	31	1-Aug	2-Aug	3-Aug

My July Routine

On Sundays, I/We:

On Mondays, I/We

On Tuesdays, I/We

On Wednesdays, I/We

On Thursdays, I/We

On Fridays, I/We

On Saturdays, I/We

My July Financial Obligations

List bills due after this paydate but before the next paydate

1st Paycheck Date_____	Bill Due Date	Bill Amount
Financial Obligation		
1		
2		
3		
4		
5		
6		
7		
8		

My July Financial Obligations

List bills due after this paydate but before the next paydate

2nd Paycheck Date_____		
Financial Obligation	**Bill Due Date**	**Bill Amount**
9		
10		
11		
12		
13		
14		
15		
16		

My July Financial Obligations

List bills due after this paydate but before the next paydate

3rd Paycheck Date_____	Bill Due Date	Bill Amount
Financial Obligation		
1		
2		
3		
4		
5		
6		
7		
8		

My July Financial Obligations

List bills due after this paydate but before the next paydate

4th Paycheck Date_____	Bill Due Date	Bill Amount
Financial Obligation		
9		
10		
11		
12		
13		
14		
15		
16		

July Meal Planner

	Breakfast or Brunch	Lunch	Afternoon Snack	Dinner
1-Jul				
2-Jul				
3-Jul				
4-Jul				
5-Jul				
6-Jul				
7-Jul				
8-Jul				
9-Jul				
10-Jul				
11-Jul				
12-Jul				

July Meal Planner

	Breakfast or Brunch	Lunch	Afternoon Snack	Dinner
13-Jul				
14-Jul				
15-Jul				
16-Jul				
17-Jul				
18-Jul				
19-Jul				
20-Jul				
21-Jul				
22-Jul				
23-Jul				
24-Jul				

July Meal Planner

	Breakfast or Brunch	Lunch	Afternoon Snack	Dinner
25-Jul				
26-Jul				
27-Jul				
28-Jul				
29-Jul				
30-Jul				
31-Jul				

My July First Paycheck Shopping List

Household Products	Personal Products	Ingredients for Planned Meals

My July Second Paycheck Shopping List

Household Products	Personal Products	Ingredients for Planned Meals

My July Third Paycheck Shopping List

Household Products	Personal Products	Ingredients for Planned Meals

My July Foure Paycheck Shopping List

Household Products	Personal Products	Ingredients for Planned Meals

July Journal Topic of the Month:

What advice about life would you like to pass on to the next generation?

_____

_____

_____

_____

_____

_____

_____

_____

_____

_____

_____

_____

_____

_____

_____

_____

_____

_____

_____

_____

My July Thoughts:

August 2024

Sunday	Monday	Tuesday	Wednesday	Thursday	Friday	Saturday
28-Jul	29-Jul	30-Jul	31-Jul	**1** Girlfriend Day <> Mahjong Day	**2** Ice Cream Sandwich Day	**3** Watermelon Day
4 Single Working Women's Day <> International Beer Day	**5** Work Like a Dog Day	**6** Sisters Day <> Fresh Breath Day	**7** Lighthouse Day	**8** Happiness Happens Day	**9** Book Lover's Day	**10** Lazy Day
11 Son & Daughter Day <> Presidential Joke Day <> Play in the Sand Day	**12** Middle Child Day	**13** Left- Hander's Day	**14** Creamsicle Day	**15** Relaxation Day	**16** National Airborne Day <> Tell a Joke Day <> Roller Coaster Day	**17** Thrift Shop Day
18 Mail Order Catalog Day	**19** Photo Day	**20** Chocolate Pecan Pie Day	**21** Leo ends <> Spumoni Day	**22** Virgo begins <> Be an Angel Day <> Tooth Fairy Day <> Never Bean Better Day	**23**	**24**
25 Kiss & Make Up Day	**26** Women's Equality Day <> Dog Appreciation Day <> Cherry Popscicle Day	**27**	**28** Bow Tie Day	**29**	**30** Frankenstein Day <> Slinky Day	**31** International Overdose Awareness Day <> Eat Outside Day

Children's Eye Health & Safety Month <> National Immunization Awareness Month

My August 2024

Sunday	Monday	Tuesday	Wednesday	Thursday	Friday	Saturday
28-Jul	29-Jul	30-Jul	31-Jul	1	2	3
4	5	6	7	8	9	10
11	12	13	14	15	16	17
18	19	20	21	22	23	24
25	26	27	28	29	30	31

My August Routine

On Sundays, I/We:

On Mondays, I/We

On Tuesdays, I/We

On Wednesdays, I/We

On Thursdays, I/We

On Fridays, I/We

On Saturdays, I/We

My August Financial Obligations

List bills due after this paydate but before the next paydate

1st Paycheck Date_____		Bill Due Date	Bill Amount
	Financial Obligation		
1			
2			
3			
4			
5			
6			
7			
8			

My August Financial Obligations

List bills due after this paydate but before the next paydate

2nd Paycheck Date_____		Bill Due Date	Bill Amount
	Financial Obligation		
9			
10			
11			
12			
13			
14			
15			
16			

My August Financial Obligations

List bills due after this paydate but before the next paydate

3rd Paycheck Date_____			Bill Due Date	Bill Amount
	Financial Obligation			
1				
2				
3				
4				
5				
6				
7				
8				

My August Financial Obligations

List bills due after this paydate but before the next paydate

4th Paycheck Date_____			Bill Due Date	Bill Amount
	Financial Obligation			
9				
10				
11				
12				
13				
14				
15				
16				

August Meal Planner

	Breakfast or Brunch	Lunch	Afternoon Snack	Dinner
1-Aug				
2-Aug				
3-Aug				
4-Aug				
5-Aug				
6-Aug				
7-Aug				
8-Aug				
9-Aug				
10-Aug				
11-Aug				
12-Aug				

August Meal Planner

	Breakfast or Brunch	Lunch	Afternoon Snack	Dinner
13-Aug				
14-Aug				
15-Aug				
16-Aug				
17-Aug				
18-Aug				
19-Aug				
20-Feb				
21-Aug				
22-Aug				
23-Aug				
24-Aug				

August Meal Planner

	Breakfast or Brunch	Lunch	Afternoon Snack	Dinner
25-Aug				
26-Aug				
27-Aug				
28-Aug				
29-Aug				
30-Aug				
31-Aug				

My August First Paycheck Shopping List

Household Products	Personal Products	Ingredients for Planned Meals

My August Second Paycheck Shopping List

Household Products	Personal Products	Ingredients for Planned Meals

My August Third Paycheck Shopping List

Household Products	Personal Products	Ingredients for Planned Meals

My Foure Foure Paycheck Shopping List

Household Products	Personal Products	Ingredients for Planned Meals

August Journal Topic of the Month:

If you could learn something new right now and then utilize the skill to earn extra money or to make a living, what would it be?

_____

_____

_____

_____

_____

_____

_____

_____

_____

_____

_____

_____

_____

_____

_____

_____

_____

_____

_____

_____

_____

My August Thoughts:

_____

_____

_____

_____

_____

_____

_____

_____

_____

_____

_____

_____

_____

_____

_____

_____

_____

_____

_____

_____

September 2024

Flower: Marigold & Cosmos   **Birthstone: Opal**

Sunday	Monday	Tuesday	Wednesday	Thursday	Friday	Saturday
1 No Rhyme or Reason Day	**2** Labor Day <> Blueberry Popsicle Day	**3** Skyscraper Day	**4** World Sexual Health Day <> Eat An Extra Dessert Day	**5** National Suicide Prevention Week (5th - 11th) <> Cheese Pizza Day	**6** Fight Procrastination Day <> Read a Book Day	**7** National Days of Prayer & Remembrance <> Salami Day
8 Grandparents' Day * National Days of Prayer & Remembrance <> Pardon	**9** Sudoku Day	**10** Hug Your Hound Day <> Swap Ideas Day	**11** Emergency Number Day <> Make Your Bed Day	**12** Internatonal Programmers Day <> Video Games Day <> Chocolate Milkshake	**13** *Friday the 13th* <> Roald Dahl Day <> Positive Thinking Day	**14**
15 Make a Hat Day	**16** Play-Doh Day <> Guacamole Day <> Collect Rocks Day <> Clean-Up Day	**17** Constitution Day <> Constitution Week <> Citizenship Day <> Country Music Day	**18** Rice Krispies Treats Day	**19** Talk Like a Pirate Day <> Gymnastics Day	**20** National POW/MIA Recognition Day <> Punch Day	**21** Virgo ends <> Big Whopper Liar Day <> Miniture Golf Day <> Dance Day
22 Autumn Equinox <> American Business Women's Day <> Libra begins	**23** Family Day <> Checkers Day <> Astronomy Day	**24** Punctuation Day	**25** Comic Book Day	**26** Love Note Day	**27** Crush a Can Day	**28** Good Neighbor Day <> World Rabies Day <> Ask a Stupid Question Day
29 World Heart Day	**30** Chewing Gum Day <> Hot Mulled Cider Day	**1-Oct**	**2-Oct**	**3-Oct**	**4-Oct**	**5-Oct**

Gospel Music Heritage Month <> National African Immigrant Heritage Month <> National Bourbon Heritage Month <> National Childhood Cancer Awareness Month <> National Guide Dog Month <> National Hispanic Heritage Month (Sept 15th - October 15th) <> National Honey Month <> National Preparedness Month <> National Prostate Health Month <> National Yoga Month <> Pain Awareness Month <> Reye's Syndrome Awareness Month <> Suicide Prevention Month <> Blood Cancer Awareness Month <> National Childhood Obesity Awareness Month <> Sickle Cell Awareness Month <> Sepsis Awareness Month

My September 2024

Sunday	Monday	Tuesday	Wednesday	Thursday	Friday	Saturday
1	2	3	4	5	6	7
8	9	10	11	12	13	14
15	16	17	18	19	20	21
22	23	24	25	26	27	28
29	30	1-Oct	2-Oct	3-Oct	4-Oct	5-Oct

My September Routine

On Sundays, I/We:

On Mondays, I/We

On Tuesdays, I/We

On Wednesdays, I/We

On Thursdays, I/We

On Fridays, I/We

On Saturdays, I/We

My September Financial Obligations

List bills due after this paydate but before the next paydate

1st Paycheck Date_____	Bill Due Date	Bill Amount
Financial Obligation		
1		
2		
3		
4		
5		
6		
7		
8		

My September Financial Obligations

List bills due after this paydate but before the next paydate

2nd Paycheck Date_____	Bill Due Date	Bill Amount
Financial Obligation		
9		
10		
11		
12		
13		
14		
15		
16		

My September Financial Obligations

List bills due after this paydate but before the next paydate

3rd Paycheck Date_____	Bill Due Date	Bill Amount
Financial Obligation		
1		
2		
3		
4		
5		
6		
7		
8		

My September Financial Obligations

List bills due after this paydate but before the next paydate

4th Paycheck Date_____	Bill Due Date	Bill Amount
Financial Obligation		
9		
10		
11		
12		
13		
14		
15		
16		

September Meal Planner

	Breakfast or Brunch	Lunch	Afternoon Snack	Dinner
1-Sep				
2-Sep				
3-Sep				
4-Sep				
5-Sep				
6-Sep				
7-Sep				
8-Sep				
9-Sep				
10-Sep				
11-Sep				
12-Sep				

September Meal Planner

	Breakfast or Brunch	Lunch	Afternoon Snack	Dinner
13-Sep				
14-Sep				
15-Sep				
16-Sep				
17-Sep				
18-Sep				
19-Sep				
20-Sep				
21-Sep				
22-Sep				
23-Sep				
24-Sep				

September Meal Planner

	Breakfast or Brunch	Lunch	Afternoon Snack	Dinner
25-Sep				
26-Sep				
27-Sep				
28-Sep				
29-Sep				
30-Sep				

My September First Paycheck Shopping List

Household Products	Personal Products	Ingredients for Planned Meals

My September Second Paycheck Shopping List

Household Products	Personal Products	Ingredients for Planned Meals

My September Third Paycheck Shopping List

Household Products	Personal Products	Ingredients for Planned Meals

My September Foure Paycheck Shopping List

Household Products	Personal Products	Ingredients for Planned Meals

September Journal Topic of the Month:

What is your favorite charitable organization and why?

_____

_____

_____

_____

_____

_____

_____

_____

_____

_____

_____

_____

_____

_____

_____

_____

_____

_____

_____

My September Thoughts:

_____

_____

_____

_____

_____

_____

_____

_____

_____

_____

_____

_____

_____

_____

_____

_____

_____

_____

_____

_____

_____

October 2024

Flowers: Marigold & Cosmos **Birthstone: Opal**

Sunday	Monday	Tuesday	Wednesday	Thursday	Friday	Saturday
29-Sep	30-Sep	**1** Vegetarian Day <> Coffee Day <> Balloons Around the World Day	**2**	**3** Mental Illness Awareness Week (3rd - 9th)	**4** Malnutrition Awareness Week (4th - 8th) <> Taco Day	**5** National Depression Screening Day
6 German-American Day <> World Cerebral Palsy Day <> Smile Day <> Mad Hatter Day	**7** Child Health Day <> National Depression Screening Day <> Card Making Day <> Frappe Day	**8** Pierogi Day	**9** Curious Events Day	**10** World Mental Health Day <> World Sight Day <> Handbag Day	**11** It's My Party Day	**12** Old Farmer's Day
13 Clergy Appreciation Day <> Skeptics Day	**14** Columbus Day	**15** White Cane Safety Day <> I Love Lucy Day	**16** Boss' Day <> Columbus Day <> Dictionary Day	**17** Wear Something Gawdy Day	**18** Chocolate Cupcake Day	**19** Sweetest Day
20 Sloth Day	**21** Libra ends <> Count Your Buttons Day	**22** Scorpio begins <> Caps Lock Day	**23** Mole Day	**24** United Nations Day <> Bologna Day	**25** Sourest Day	**26** Howl at the Moon Day & Night
27 American Beer Day	**28** Animation Day	**29** World Stroke Day <> Internet Day	**30** Candy Corn Day	**31** **Halloween** <> Magic Day <> Knock-Knock Jokes Day	1-Nov	2-Nov

Breast Cancer Awareness Month <> Filipino-American Heritage & Culture Month <> Italian-American Heritage & Culture Month <> National Arts & Humanities Month <> National Cyber Security Awareness Month <> National Disability Employment Awareness Month <> National Hispanic Heritage Month (Sept 15th - Oct 15th) <> National Pizza Month <> National Work & Family Month <> Polish-American Heritage Month <> National ADHD Awareness Month <> National Down Syndrome Awareness Month <> National Physical Therapy Month <> Pregnancy & Infant Loss Awareness Month <> Spina Bifida Awareness Month <> SIDS Awareness Month

My October 2024

Sunday	Monday	Tuesday	Wednesday	Thursday	Friday	Saturday
1	2	3	4	5	6	7
8	9	10	11	12	13	14
15	16	17	18	19	20	21
22	23	24	25	26	27	28
29	30	31	1-Nov	2-Nov	3-Nov	4-Nov

My October Routine

On Sundays, I/We:

On Mondays, I/We

On Tuesdays, I/We

On Wednesdays, I/We

On Thursdays, I/We

On Fridays, I/We

On Saturdays, I/We

My October Financial Obligations

List bills due after this paydate but before the next paydate

1st Paycheck Date_____	Bill Due Date	Bill Amount
Financial Obligation		
1		
2		
3		
4		
5		
6		
7		
8		

My October Financial Obligations

List bills due after this paydate but before the next paydate

2nd Paycheck Date_____	Bill Due Date	Bill Amount
Financial Obligation		
9		
10		
11		
12		
13		
14		
15		
16		

My October Financial Obligations

List bills due after this paydate but before the next paydate

3rd Paycheck Date_____	Bill Due Date	Bill Amount
Financial Obligation		
1		
2		
3		
4		
5		
6		
7		
8		

My October Financial Obligations

List bills due after this paydate but before the next paydate

4th Paycheck Date_____	Bill Due Date	Bill Amount
Financial Obligation		
9		
10		
11		
12		
13		
14		
15		
16		

October Meal Planner

	Breakfast or Brunch	Lunch	Afternoon Snack	Dinner
1-Oct				
2-Oct				
3-Oct				
4-Oct				
5-Oct				
6-Oct				
7-Oct				
8-Oct				
9-Oct				
10-Oct				
11-Oct				
12-Oct				

October Meal Planner

	Breakfast or Brunch	Lunch	Afternoon Snack	Dinner
13-Oct				
14-Oct				
15-Oct				
16-Oct				
17-Oct				
18-Oct				
19-Oct				
20-Oct				
21-Oct				
22-Oct				
23-Oct				
24-Oct				

October Meal Planner

	Breakfast or Brunch	Lunch	Afternoon Snack	Dinner
25-Oct				
26-Oct				
27-Oct				
28-Oct				
29-Oct				
30-Oct				
31-Oct				

My October First Paycheck Shopping List

Household Products	Personal Products	Ingredients for Planned Meals

My October Second Paycheck Shopping List

Household Products	Personal Products	Ingredients for Planned Meals

My October Third Paycheck Shopping List

Household Products	Personal Products	Ingredients for Planned Meals

My October Foure Paycheck Shopping List

Household Products	Personal Products	Ingredients for Planned Meals

October Journal Topic of the Month:

Describe a dream of yours that has not come true yet?

_____

_____

_____

_____

_____

_____

_____

_____

_____

_____

_____

_____

_____

_____

_____

_____

_____

_____

_____

_____

_____

My October Thoughts:

_____

_____

_____

_____

_____

_____

_____

_____

_____

_____

_____

_____

_____

_____

_____

_____

_____

_____

_____

_____

_____

November 2024

Chrysanthemum   Birthstone

Sunday	Monday	Tuesday	Wednesday	Thursday	Friday	Saturday
27-Oct	28-Oct	29-Oct	30-Oct	31-Oct	**1** Vegan Day <> Jersey Friday <> Author's Day	**2** Devilled Eggs Day <> Men Make Dinner Day <> Stout Day
3 Transgender Awareness Week <> Daylight Savings Time ends <> Sandwich Day	**4** Common Sense Day	**5** **Election Day** <> Zero Tasking Day	**6** Saxophone Day	**7** Hug a Bear Day <> Bittersweet Chocolate W/Almonds Day	**8** Tongue Twister Day	**9** World Freedom Day <> Chaos Never Dies Day
10 Forget-Me-Nots Day <> Vanilla Cupcakes Day	**11** **Veteran's Day** <> Origami Day	**12** World Pneumonia Day <> Happy Hour Day	**13** World Kindness Day <> Sadie Hawkins Day	**14** Spicy Guacamole Day <> Pickle Day	**15** National Philanthropy Day <> America Recycles Day <> Clean Out your Refridgerator Day	**16** Have a Party with Your Bear Day <> Fast Food Day <> Use Less Stuff Day
17 World Prematurity Day <> Take a Hike Day	**18** Princess Day <> Push Button Phone Day	**19** International Men's Day <> Play Monopoly Day	**20** Scorpio ends <>Absurdity Day	**21** Sagittarius begins <> Hello Day	**22** Go For A Ride Day	**23**
24 Celebrate Your Unique Talent	**25** Shopping Reminder Day	**26** Cake Day	**27**	**28** **Thanksgiving Day** <> Red Planet Day	**29** Native American Heritage Day <> *Black Friday* <> Electric Greeting Card Day	**30** Computer Security Day

National Epilepsy Awareness Month <> Academic Writing Month <> American Diabetes Month <> Black Catholic History Month <> COPD Awareness Month <> Movember <> National Novel Writing Month <> Native American Indian & Alaskan Native Heritage Month <> Bladder Health Month <> Diabetic Eye Disease Month <> Lung Cancer Awareness Month <> National Healthy Skin Month <> National Hospice & Palliative Care Month <> National Stomach Cancer Awareness Month <> Pancreatic Cancer Awareness Month <> Prematurity Awareness Month <>

My November 2024

Sunday	Monday	Tuesday	Wednesday	Thursday	Friday	Saturday
27-Oct	28-Oct	29-Oct	30-Oct	31-Oct	1	2
3	4	5	6	7	8	9
10	11	12	13	14	15	16
17	18	19	20	21	22	23
24	25	26	27	28	29	30

My November Routine

On Sundays, I/We:

On Mondays, I/We

On Tuesdays, I/We

On Wednesdays, I/We

On Thursdays, I/We

On Fridays, I/We

On Saturdays, I/We

My November Financial Obligations

List bills due after this paydate but before the next paydate

1st Paycheck Date_____	Bill Due Date	Bill Amount
Financial Obligation		
1		
2		
3		
4		
5		
6		
7		
8		

My November Financial Obligations

List bills due after this paydate but before the next paydate

2nd Paycheck Date_____	Bill Due Date	Bill Amount
Financial Obligation		
9		
10		
11		
12		
13		
14		
15		
16		

My November Financial Obligations

List bills due after this paydate but before the next paydate

3rd Paycheck Date_____	Bill Due Date	Bill Amount
Financial Obligation		
1		
2		
3		
4		
5		
6		
7		
8		

My November Financial Obligations

List bills due after this paydate but before the next paydate

4th Paycheck Date_____	Bill Due Date	Bill Amount
Financial Obligation		
9		
10		
11		
12		
13		
14		
15		
16		

November Meal Planner

	Breakfast or Brunch	Lunch	Afternoon Snack	Dinner
1-Nov				
2-Nov				
3-Nov				
4-Nov				
5-Nov				
6-Nov				
7-Nov				
8-Nov				
9-Nov				
10-Nov				
11-Nov				
12-Nov				

November Meal Planner

	Breakfast or Brunch	Lunch	Afternoon Snack	Dinner
13-Nov				
14-Nov				
15-Nov				
16-Nov				
17-Nov				
18-Nov				
19-Nov				
20-Nov				
21-Nov				
22-Nov				
23-Nov				
24-Nov				

November Meal Planner

	Breakfast or Brunch	Lunch	Afternoon Snack	Dinner
25-Nov				
26-Nov				
27-Nov				
28-Nov				
29-Nov				
30-Nov				

My November First Paycheck Shopping List

Household Products	Personal Products	Ingredients for Planned Meals

My November Second Paycheck Shopping List

Household Products	Personal Products	Ingredients for Planned Meals

My November Third Paycheck Shopping List

Household Products	Personal Products	Ingredients for Planned Meals

My November Fourth Paycheck Shopping List

Household Products	Personal Products	Ingredients for Planned Meals

November Journal Topic of the Month:
choose your topic
What am I thankful for? -or- What is your favorite part of the
Thanksgiving Holiday?-or- Choose a holiday or common celebratio
and then upgrade or overhaul it.

_____

_____

_____

_____

_____

_____

_____

_____

_____

_____

_____

_____

_____

_____

_____

_____

_____

_____

_____

_____

My November Thoughts:

December 2024

Flowers: Holly & Poinsetta   **Birthstone: Turquoise & Narcissus**

Sunday	Monday	Tuesday	Wednesday	Thursday	Friday	Saturday
1 World AIDS Day <> National Handwashing Awareness Week (1st - 7th) <> Eat a Red Apple Day	**2** Fritters Day	**3** International Day of Persons w/Disabilities <> Make a Gift Day	**4** Dice Day <> Wear Brown Shoes Day	**5** Bathtub Party Day <> Day of the Ninja	**6** Put on Your Own Shoes Day <> Microwave Oven Day	**7** National Pearl Harbor Remembrance Day <> Letter Writing Day
8 Pretend to Be a Time Traveler Day <> Lost & Found Day	**9** Christmas Card Day	**10** Human Rights Day & Human Rights Week <> Dewey Decimal System Day	**11** Noodle Ring Day	**12** Gingerbread House Day	**13** *Fiday the 13Th*	**14** Monkey Day
15 **Bill of Rights Day** <> Underdog Day	**16** Chocolate Covered Anything Day	**17** Wright Brother's Day	**18**	**19**	**20** Saggitarius ends <> Games Day <> Ugly Christmas Sweater Day <> Sangria Day	**21** *Winter Solstice* <> Capricorn begins <> Crossword Puzzle Day
22 Date Nut Bread Day	**23**	**24** Egg Nog Day	**25** **Christmas**	**26** Thank You Note Day	**27** No Interruptions Day	**28** Card Playing Day <> Pepper Pot Day
29	**30** Bicarbonate of Soda Day	**31** New Year's Eve <> Make Up Your Mind Day	1-Jan	2-Jan	3-Jan	4-Jan

There are no awareness celebrations for the month of December.

My December 2024

Sunday	Monday	Tuesday	Wednesday	Thursday	Friday	Saturday
1	2	3	4	5	6	7
8	9	10	11	12	13	14
15	16	17	18	19	20	21
22	23	24	25	26	27	28
29	30	31	1-Jan	2-Jan	3-Jan	4-Jan

My December Routine

On Sundays, I/We:

On Mondays, I/We

On Tuesdays, I/We

On Wednesdays, I/We

On Thursdays, I/We

On Fridays, I/We

On Saturdays, I/We

My December Financial Obligations

List bills due after this paydate but before the next paydate

1st Paycheck Date_____	Bill Due Date	Bill Amount
Financial Obligation		
1		
2		
3		
4		
5		
6		
7		
8		

My December Financial Obligations

List bills due after this paydate but before the next paydate

2nd Paycheck Date_____	Bill Due Date	Bill Amount
Financial Obligation		
9		
10		
11		
12		
13		
14		
15		
16		

My December Financial Obligations

List bills due after this paydate but before the next paydate

3rd Paycheck Date_____	Bill Due Date	Bill Amount
Financial Obligation		
1		
2		
3		
4		
5		
6		
7		
8		

My December Financial Obligations

List bills due after this paydate but before the next paydate

4th Paycheck Date_____	Bill Due Date	Bill Amount
Financial Obligation		
9		
10		
11		
12		
13		
14		
15		
16		

December Meal Planner

	Breakfast or Brunch	Lunch	Afternoon Snack	Dinner
1-Dec				
2-Dec				
3-Dec				
4-Dec				
5-Dec				
6-Dec				
7-Dec				
8-Dec				
9-Dec				
10-Dec				
11-Dec				
12-Dec				

December Meal Planner

	Breakfast or Brunch	Lunch	Afternoon Snack	Dinner
13-Dec				
14-Dec				
15-Dec				
16-Dec				
17-Dec				
18-Dec				
19-Dec				
20-Dec				
21-Dec				
22-Dec				
23-Dec				
24-Dec				

December Meal Planner

	Breakfast or Brunch	Lunch	Afternoon Snack	Dinner
25-Dec				
26-Dec				
27-Dec				
28-Dec				
29-Dec				
30-Dec				
31-Dec				

My December First Paycheck Shopping List

Household Products	Personal Products	Ingredients for Planned Meals

My December Second Paycheck Shopping List

Household Products	Personal Products	Ingredients for Planned Meals

My December Third Paycheck Shopping List

Household Products	Personal Products	Ingredients for Planned Meals

My December Foure Paycheck Shopping List

Household Products	Personal Products	Ingredients for Planned Meals

December Journal Topic of the Month:

What would be the best gift you could give to the world today?

_____

_____

_____

_____

_____

_____

_____

_____

_____

_____

_____

_____

_____

_____

_____

_____

_____

_____

_____

My December Thoughts:

_____

_____

_____

_____

_____

_____

_____

_____

_____

_____

_____

_____

_____

_____

_____

_____

_____

_____

_____

_____

www.ingramcontent.com/pod-product-compliance
Lightning Source LLC
Chambersburg PA
CBHW080957120626
46546CB00010B/2928